TONGUE TWISTERS

TABLE OF CONTENTS

HOW TO USE TONGUE TWISTERS

Welcome to the wacky world of tongue twisters!

Tongue twisters are a lot of fun.

They are also a great way to practice saying difficult sounds, warming up for singing and speech, and even learning new words.

Some tongue twisters are very short:

Truly rural

While others can be much longer, such as the classic "How much wood would a woodchuck chuck."

(Both of these and many many more are included in this collection. In fact, there are hundreds of tongue twisters for you to tie your tongue on in the following pages.)

Here are some tips that will help you get the most out of tongue twisters:

1. Practice saying difficult tongue twisters slowly to get accurate.
2. Speed up your delivery once you can say the tongue twisters with accuracy.
3. Once you master a tongue twister, for an extra challenge, practice saying it multiple times in a row.
4. If one tongue twister is easy, try to find another one with different sounds.
5. Once you get good at tongue twisters, try making your own: focus on repeating consonant and/or vowel sounds. And make them funny!

EASY TONGUE TWISTERS

Eleven benevolent elephants.

She sees cheese.

Six sticky skeletons.

A proper copper coffee pot.

Truly rural.

Swan swam over the sea.

Which witch is which?

Elizabeth has eleven elves
in her elm tree.

Willy's real rear wheel.

Six sleek swans
swam swiftly southwards.

Scissors sizzle, thistles sizzle.

Seventy-seven
benevolent elephants.

A happy hippo
hopped and hiccuped.

Cooks cook cupcakes quickly.

Really leery, rarely Larry.

I saw a saw that could
out-saw any other saw I ever saw.

Twelve twins
twirled twelve twigs.

A snake sneaks
to seek a snack.

Six Czech cricket critics.

Sheena leads, Sheila needs.

Blue bluebird.

Red lorry, yellow lorry.

Daddy Draws Doors.

Willie feels really weary.

Three free throws.

The big bug bit the little beetle.

Friendly fleas and fireflies.

Clean clams crammed
in clean cans.

Fresh fried fish.

Specific Pacific.

Rubber baby buggy bumpers.

Santa's short suit shrunk.

On a lazy laser raiser
lies a laser ray eraser.

Pirates Private Property

Ann and Andy's anniversary
is in April.

Rudder valve reversals

So, this is the sushi chef!

Three short sword sheaths.

Tie twine to three tree twigs.

Six sing-along-songs.

Rolling red wagons

The queen in green screamed.

She threw three balls.

I wish to wash
my Irish wristwatch.

Unique New York.

Tom threw Tim three thumbtacks.

He threw three free throws.

Fresh French fried fly fritters.

Gig whip, gig whip, gig whip.

Eddie edited it.

Two tiny tigers
take two taxis to town.

I wish you were a fish in my dish.

A gazillion gigantic grapes
gushed gradually,
giving gophers gooey guts.

Silly sheep weep and sleep.

Bake big batches
of bitter brown bread.

Pay the purple people eater.

Busy buzzing bumble bees.

A lump of red leather,
a red leather lump

I saw a kitten
eating chicken in the kitchen.

Nine nice night nurses
nursing nicely.

She sells sea shells by the seashore.

Shave a single shingle thin.

Crisp crusts crackle and crunch.

Round the rugged rocks
the ragged rascals ran.

The cat catchers
can't catch caught cats.

Three fluffy feathers
fell from Phoebe's flimsy fan.

She should shun the shining sun.

Cooks cook cupcakes quickly.

Betty and Bob
brought back blue balloons
from the big bazaar.

Little Lillian lets lazy lizards
lie along the lily pads

Each Easter Eddie eats
eighty Easter eggs.

Red lorry, yellow lorry

Sheep should sleep in a shed.

Zebras zig and zebras zag.

The blue bluebird blinks.

Four fine fresh fish for you.

He threw three balls.

Lucky rabbits
like to cause a ruckus.

A big black bear
sat on a big black rug.

Kitty caught the kitten
in the kitchen.

We surely shall see
the sunshine soon.

Four furious friends
fought for the phone.

Dewdrops drops.

Stash of pistashios.

Two tried and true tridents.

Flash message.

Selfish shellfish.

Greet with glee.

World Wide Web.

What a terrible tongue twister.

Caution: Wide Right Turns.

Salty broccoli.

Are our oars oak?

A cheap ship trip.

Draw drowsy ducks and drakes.

Pure food for poor mules.

Shredded Swiss cheese.

Thin sticks, thin bricks.

Local cola.

Lakota koala.

MEDIUM TONGUE TWISTERS

Fred fed Ted bread
and Ted fed Fred bread.

Betty's big bunny
bobbled by the blueberry bush.

Green glass globes glow greenly.

A big bug bit the little beetle
but the little beetle
bit the big bug back.

Of all the smells I have ever smelt,
I never smelt a smell
that smelt like that smell smelt.

Top chopstick shops
stock top chopsticks.

Two tiny timid toads
trying to trot to Tarrytown.

Ingenious iguanas improvising
an intricate impromptu on
impossibly-impractical instruments.

Sounding by sound
is a sound method
of sounding sounds.

If a dog chews shoes,
whose shoes does he choose?

I scream, you scream,
We all scream for ice cream.

A sailor went to sea
To see, what he could see.
And all he could see
Was sea, sea, sea.

Pad kid poured
curd pulled cold.

Wayne went to
Wales to watch walruses.

Why do you cry, Willy?
Why do you cry?
Why, Willy?
Why, Willy?
Why, Willy? Why?

Six slimy snails sailed silently.

Octopus ocular optics.

How many yaks could a yak pack,
pack if a yak pack could pack yaks?

Can you can a can
as a canner can can a can?

Double bubble gum,
bubbles double.

Gobbling gargoyles gobbled
gobbling goblins.

I slit the sheet, the sheet I slit,
and on the slitted sheet I sit.

Six sick hicks nick six slick bricks
with picks and sticks.

Can you can a canned can into
an un-canned can like a canner
can can a canned can
into an un-canned can?

Fuzzy Wuzzy was a bear.
Fuzzy Wuzzy had no hair.
Fuzzy Wuzzy wasn't fuzzy, was he?

A flea and a fly flew up in a flue.

Susie's sister
sewed socks for soldiers.

An ape hates grape cakes.

Imagine an imaginary
menagerie manager managing an
imaginary menagerie.

Rory the warrior
and Roger the worrier
were reared wrongly
in a rural brewery.

Send toast to ten tense stout saints'
ten tall tents.

Denise sees the fleece,
Denise sees the fleas.
At least Denise could sneeze
And feed and freeze the fleas.

Any noise annoys an oyster
but a noisy noise
annoys an oyster more.

If a black bug bleeds black blood,
what color blood
does a blue bug bleed?

If two witches were
watching two watches:
which witch would watch
which watch?

Rory's lawn rake
rarely rakes really right.

Wanting won't win;
winning ways are active ways.

Seventeen sales slips
slithered slowly southwards.

Feel free to follow that fellow.

Ensuring excellence isn't easy.

She sold six
shabby sheared sheep on ship.

Mix a box of mixed biscuits
with a boxed biscuit mixer.

If you notice this notice,
you will notice that this notice
is not worth noticing.

The bottom of the butter bucket
is the buttered bucket bottom.

Vincent vowed vengeance
very vehemently.

Does your sport shop
stock short socks with spots?

Many mumbling mice
are making merry music
in the moonlight.

The boot black brought
the black boot back.

No need to light a night-light
on a light night like tonight.

"These sheaths," she seethed,
"were seized by thieves."

I saw Susie sitting
in a shoe shine shop.

A big black bug
bit a big black bear
made the big black bear
bleed blood.

Rural Juror.

The sixth sick sheik's
sixth sheep's sick.

Kindly kittens knitting mittens
keep kazooing in the king's kitchen.

A skunk sat on a stump
and thunk the stump stunk,
but the stump thunk
the skunk stunk.

Lesser leather never weathered
wetter weather better.

She saw Sharif's shoes on the sofa.
But was she so sure
those were Sharif's shoes she saw?

The thirty-three thieves
thought that they thrilled
the throne throughout Thursday.

Roberta ran rings
around the Roman ruins.

If Stu chews shoes,
should Stu choose
the shoes he chews?

There those thousand thinkers
were thinking how did the other
three thieves go through.

One-one was a race horse.
Two-two was one too.
One-one won one race.
Two-two won one too.

Bread spreaders spread bread,
bed spreaders spread beds.

When you write copy
you have the right to copyright
the copy you write.

A big black bug bit a big black dog
on his big black nose!

Hassock hassock,
black spotted hassock.
Black spot on a black back
of a black spotted hassock.

Seven slick slimey snakes
slowly sliding southward.

Roofs of mushrooms
rarely mush too much.

The great Greek grape growers
grow great Greek grapes.

Singing Sammy sung songs
on sinking sand.

Rhys watched Ross switch his Irish
wristwatch for a Swiss wristwatch.

The ruddy widow really wants
ripe watermelon and red roses
when winter arrives.

If you're keen on stunning kites
and cunning stunts,
buy a cunning stunning stunt kite.

Tommy Tucker tried to tie
Tammy's Turtles tie.

Suzie Seaword's fish-sauce shop
sells unsifted thistles
for thistle-sifters to sift.

Seven sleazy shysters
in sharkskin suits
sold sheared sealskins
to seasick sailors.

Knife and a fork,
bottle and a cork
that is the way you spell New York.

Chicken in the car,
and the car can go,
that is the way you spell Chicago.

Five fuzzy French frogs
frolicked through the fields
in France.

Round and round the rugged rock
the ragged rascal ran.

Thirty-three thousand people
think that Thursday
is their thirtieth birthday.

Shut up the shutters
and sit in the shop.

How many snacks
could a snack stacker stack,
if a snack stacker
snacked stacked snacks?

Five frantic frogs fled
from fifty fierce fishes.

If practice makes perfect
and perfect needs practice,
I'm perfectly practiced
and practically perfect.

A bragging baker
baked black bread.

These sheep
shouldn't sleep in a shack;
Sheep should sleep in a shed.

Silly Sally swiftly shooed
seven silly sheep.
The seven silly sheep
Silly Sally shooed
Shilly-shallied south.

Susie works in a shoeshine shop.
Where she shines, she sits,
and where she sits, she shines.

Red Buick, blue Buick

Rugged rubber
baby buggy bumpers.

Three grey geese in
green fields grazing.

How many boards
Could the Mongols hoard
If the Mongol hordes got bored?

Comical economists.

Frogfeet, flippers, swimfins.

Elizabeth's birthday is on the third Thursday of this month.

A shapeless sash sags slowly.

Smelly shoes
and socks shock sisters.

Supposed to be pistachio

Argyle Gargoyle

Casual clothes are provisional
for leisurely trips across Asia.

Shoulder surgery.

A box of biscuits,
a batch of mixed biscuits.

Brad's big black bath brush broke.

Cecily thought Sicily
less thistly than Thessaly.

Cedar shingles
should be shaved and saved.

Don't pamper damp scamp tramps
that camp under ramp lamps.

The crow flew over the river
with a lump of raw liver.

Crisp crusts crackle crunchily.

Cows graze in groves on grass
which grows in grooves in groves.

Chop shops stock chops.

The epitome of femininity.

Fat frogs flying past fast.

A fat thrush flies through thick fog.

Gertie's great-grandma
grew aghast at Gertie's grammar.

I correctly recollect
Rebecca MacGregor's reckoning.

I can think of six thin things
and of six thick things too.

Friendly Frank flips fine flapjacks.

Many an anemone
sees an enemy anemone.

Lovely lemon liniment

Listen to the local yokel yodel.

Lily ladles little Letty's lentil soup.

A laurel-crowned clown

Moose noshing much mush

Old oily Ollie oils old oily autos.

Pacific Lithograph

Plague-bearing prairie dogs.

Pick a partner and practice passing,
for if you pass proficiently,
perhaps you'll play professionally.

A pleasant place to place a plaice
is a place where a plaice
is pleased to be placed.

Shy Shelly says
she shall sew sheets.

Six sharp smart sharks.

HARD
TONGUE
TWISTERS

Peter Piper picked a peck of pickled peppers;
A peck of pickled peppers Peter Piper picked;
If Peter Piper picked a peck of pickled peppers,
Where's the peck of pickled peppers
Peter Piper picked?

How much wood would a woodchuck chuck
if a woodchuck could chuck wood?
He would chuck, he would, as much as he could,
and chuck as much wood as a woodchuck would
if a woodchuck could chuck wood.

Betty Botter bought some butter but
said she the butter's bitter.
If I put it in my batter
it will make my batter bitter.
But a bit of better butter
will make my bitter batter better.
So she bought some better butter
better than the bitter butter,
put it in her bitter batter
made her bitter batter better.
So twas better Betty Botter
bought some better butter.

She sells seashells on the seashore.
The shells she sells are seashells, I'm sure.
And if she sells seashells on the seashore,
Then I'm sure she sells seashore shells.

How much ground would a groundhog hog,
if a groundhog could hog ground?
A groundhog would hog
all the ground he could hog,
if a groundhog could hog ground.

Yellow butter, purple jelly, red jam, black bread.
Spread it thick, say it quick!
Yellow butter, purple jelly, red jam, black bread.
Spread it thicker, say it quicker!
Yellow butter, purple jelly, red jam, black bread.
Don't eat with your mouth full!

If you must cross a course cross cow
across a crowded cow crossing,
cross the cross coarse cow across
the crowded cow crossing carefully.

Brisk brave brigadiers brandished
broad bright blades, blunderbusses, and bludgeons
— balancing them badly.

To sit in solemn silence in a dull, dark dock,
In a pestilential prison, with a life-long lock,
Awaiting the sensation of a short, sharp shock,
From a cheap and chippy chopper on a big black block!

Luke Luck likes lakes.
Luke's duck likes lakes.
Luke Luck licks lakes.
Luke's duck licks lakes.
Duck takes licks in lakes Luke Luck likes.
Luke Luck takes licks in lakes duck likes.

Through three cheese trees three free fleas flew
While these fleas flew, freezy breeze blew
Freezy breeze made these three trees freeze
Freezy trees made these trees' cheese freeze
That's what made these three free fleas sneeze

Denise sees the fleece,
Denise sees the fleas.
At least Denise could sneeze
And feed and freeze the fleas.

Chester cheetah chews a chunk
of cheap cheddar cheese
If the chunk of cheese
chunked Chester cheetah,
What would Chester cheetah
chew and chunk on?

Super-duper storm troopers
whoop it up at Death Star groupers:
helmet thrashing, rebel bashing,
laser blasting at party poopers.

Thirty-three thirsty, thundering thoroughbreds
thumped Mr. Thurber on Thursday.

To begin to toboggan first buy a toboggan,
but don't buy too big a toboggan.
Too big a toboggan is too big a toboggan to buy
to begin to toboggan.

Hassock hassock, black spotted hassock.
Black spot on a black back of a black spotted hassock.

Did Dick Pickens prick his pinkie
pickling cheap cling peaches in an inch of Pinch
or framing his famed French finch photos?

I wish to wish the wish you wish to wish,
but if you wish the wish the witch wishes,
I won't wish the wish you wish to wish.

There was a fisherman named Fisher
who fished for some fish in a fissure.
Till a fish with a grin,
pulled the fisherman in.
Now they're fishing the fissure for Fisher.

Picky people pick Peter Pan Peanut-Butter,
'tis the peanut-butter picky people pick.

Luke Luck likes lakes.
Luke's duck likes lakes.
Luke Luck licks lakes.
Luck's duck licks lakes.
Duck takes licks in lakes Luke Luck likes.
Luke Luck takes licks in lakes duck likes.

How many cans can a cannibal nibble
if a cannibal can nibble cans?
As many cans as a cannibal can nibble
if a cannibal can nibble cans.

Bobby Bippy bought a bat.
Bobby Bippy bought a ball.
With his bat Bob banged the ball
Banged it bump against the wall
But so boldly Bobby banged it
That he burst his rubber ball
"Boo!" cried Bobby
Bad luck ball
Bad luck Bobby, bad luck ball
Now to drown his many troubles
Bobby Bippy's blowing bubbles.

How many berries could a bare berry carry,
if a bare berry could carry berries?
Well they can't carry berries
(which could make you very wary)
but a bare berry carried is more scary!

A fly and flea flew into a flue,
said the fly to the flea 'what shall we do?'
'let us fly' said the flea
said the fly 'shall we flee'
so they flew through a flaw in the flue.

How much dew does a dewdrop drop
If dewdrops do drop dew?
They do drop, they do
As do dewdrops drop
If dewdrops do drop dew.

If one doctor doctors another doctor,
then which doctor is doctoring the doctored doctor?
Does the doctor who doctors the doctor,
doctor the doctor the way
the doctor is doctoring doctors?

There was a fisherman named Fisher
who fished for some fish in a fissure.
Till a fish with a grin,
pulled the fisherman in.
Now they're fishing the fissure for Fisher.

How many berries could a bare berry carry,
if a bare berry could carry berries?
Well they can't carry berries
(which could make you very wary)
but a bare berry carried is more scary!

Out in the pasture the nature watcher watches the catcher.
While the catcher watches the pitcher who pitches the balls.
Whether the temperature's up or whether the temperature's down,
the nature watcher, the catcher and the pitcher are always around.
The pitcher pitches, the catcher catches and the watcher watches.
So whether the temperature's rises or whether the temperature falls
the nature watcher just watches the catcher
who's watching the pitcher who's watching the balls.

I cannot bear to see a bear
Bear down upon a hare.
When bare of hair he strips the hare,
Right there I cry, "Forbear!"

If a Hottentot taught a Hottentot tot
To talk ere the tot could totter,
Ought the Hottenton tot
Be taught to say aught, or naught,
Or what ought to be taught her?
If to hoot and to toot a Hottentot tot
Be taught by her Hottentot tutor,
Ought the tutor get hot
If the Hottentot tot
Hoot and toot at her Hottentot tutor?

I'm not the pheasant plucker,
I'm the pheasant plucker's mate.
I'm only plucking pheasants
'Cause the pheasant plucker's late.

I need not your needles, they're needless to me;
For kneading of noodles, 'twere needless, you see;
But did my neat knickers but need to be kneed,
I then should have need of your needles indeed.

I thought a thought
But the thought I thought
Was not the thought
I thought I thought.

Mr. See owned a saw.
And Mr. Soar owned a seesaw.
Now See's saw sawed Soar's seesaw
Before Soar saw See,
Which made Soar sore.
Had Soar seen See's saw
Before See sawed Soar's seesaw,
See's saw would not have sawed
Soar's seesaw.
So See's saw sawed Soar's seesaw.
But it was sad to see Soar so sore
Just because See's saw sawed
Soar's seesaw!

Ned Nott was shot and Sam Shott was not.
So it is better to be Shott than Nott.
Some say Nott was not shot.
But Shott says he shot Nott.
Either the shot Shott shot at Nott was not shot,
Or Nott was shot.
If the shot Shott shot shot Nott, Nott was shot.
But if the shot Shott shot shot Shott,
Then Shott was shot, not Nott.
However, the shot Shott shot shot not Shott, but Nott.

Once upon a barren moor
There dwelt a bear, also a boar.
The bear could not bear the boar.
The boar thought the bear a bore.
At last the bear could bear no more
Of that boar that bored him on the moor,
And so one morn he bored the boar -
That boar will bore the bear no more.

On mules we find two legs behind
And two we find before.
We stand behind before we find
What those behind be for.

Sarah saw a shot-silk sash shop
full of shot-silk sashes
as the sunshine shone on the sid
of the shot-silk sash shop.

When a twister a-twisting will twist him a twist,
For the twisting a twist, he three twines will entwist;
But if one of the twines of the twist do untwist,
The twine that untwisteth untwisteth the twist.

You've no need to light a night-light
On a light night like tonight,
For a night-light's light's a slight light,
And tonight's a night that's light.
When a night's light, like tonight's light,
It is really not quite right
To light night-lights with their slight lights
On a light night like tonight.

I am the very model of a modern Major-General,
I've information vegetable, animal, and mineral,
I know the kings of England, and I quote the fights historical
From Marathon to Waterloo, in order categorical;

I'm very well acquainted, too, with matters mathematical,
I understand equations, both the simple and quadratical,
About binomial theorem I'm teeming with a lot o' news,
Hmmm... lot o' news, lot o'news... Aha!
With many cheerful facts about the square of the hypotenuse.

I'm very good at integral and differential calculus;
I know the scientific names of beings animalculous:
In short, in matters vegetable, animal, and mineral,
I am the very model of a modern Major-General.

I know our mythic history, King Arthur's and Sir Caradoc's;
I answer hard acrostics, I've a pretty taste for paradox,
I quote in elegiacs all the crimes of Heliogabalus,
In conics I can floor peculiarities parabolous

I can tell undoubted Raphaels from Gerard Dows and Zoffanies,
I know the croaking from The Frogs of Aristophanes!
Then I can hum a fugue of which I've heard the music's din afore,
Hmmm... din afore, din afore... Aha!
And whistle all the airs from that infernal nonsense Pinafore.

Then I can write a washing bill in Babylonic cuneiform,
And tell you ev'ry detail of Caractacus's uniform:
In short, in matters vegetable, animal, and mineral,
I am the very model of a modern Major-General.

BONUS: MAJOR GENERAL'S SONG

Then I can write a washing bill in Babylonic cuneiform,
And tell you ev'ry detail of Caractacus's uniform:
In short, in matters vegetable, animal, and mineral,
I am the very model of a modern Major-General.

In fact, when I know what is meant by "mamelon" and "ravelin",
When I can tell at sight a Mauser rifle from a javelin,
When such affairs as sorties and surprises I'm more wary at,
And when I know precisely what is meant by "commissariat",

When I have learnt what progress has been made in modern gunnery,
When I know more of tactics than a novice in a nunnery
In short, when I've a smattering of elemental strategy
Hmmm... strategy... strategy, lategy, bategy... Aha! I have it!
You'll say a better Major-General has never sat a gee.

When I have learnt what progress has been made in modern gunnery,
When I know more of tactics than a novice in a nunnery
In short, when I've a smattering of elemental strategy
Hmmm... strategy... strategy, lategy, bategy... Aha! I have it!
You'll say a better Major-General has never sat a gee.

For my military knowledge, though I'm plucky and adventury,
Has only been brought down to the beginning of the century;
But still, in matters vegetable, animal, and mineral,
I am the very model of a modern Major-General.

MAKE YOUR OWN
TONGUE TWISTERS!

Printed in Great Britain
by Amazon